YOU KNOW YOU'RE ANONYMOUS IN WASHINGTON WHEN...

You know you're anonymous in
Washington when . . .

. . . you're elected Vice President.

. . . you run for office unopposed
. . . and lose.

. . . you have ten pounds of crack
and Marion Barry doesn't know it.

. . . you don't have tinted windows
on your car.

. . . you vote "nay" on a bill and it passes unanimously.

. . . people you don't like don't know you don't like them.

. . . you have a healthy liver and Ted Kennedy doesn't have dibs on it.

. . . you send the President death threats and get an autographed picture in return.

. . . you have an affair and nobody cares.

. . . people think you're doing what's best for the country.

. . . nobody hates you yet.

. . . Dan Quayle adds an extra ''e''
to your name and no one makes
a fuss.

. . . your last TV appearance was on a security camera at the Museum of Natural History.

. . . you anonymously write an inside book on Washington and nobody bothers to find out who you are.

You know you're anonymous in
Washington when . . .

. . . you can go to the bathroom on the White House lawn and you're not Socks the cat.

. . . you can check into a sleazy
motel under your real name.

. . . you go to a fund-raising dinner
for the dinner.

. . . you make a ninety-nine-thousand-dollar profit in cattle futures and nobody thinks it's unusual.

. . . your housekeeper speaks
fluent English.

. . . the only security you have is for
your car.

. . . the only Cabinet member you know is Johnnie Walker Red.

. . . during interviews people tell you the truth.

. . . you can lose an election to Michael Dukakis.

. . . you're a woman with a heartbeat and Bob Packwood doesn't make a pass at you.

. . . you give a death-row inmate a stay of execution and they kill him anyway.

. . . you run for office and no one asks to see your tax returns.

. . . the only speed dial you have on your phone is for Domino's Pizza.

. . . the only TV program you're invited to be on is "Wheel of Fortune."

. . . your campaign manager has a night job.

. . . people you interview are willing to go "on the record."

You know you're anonymous in
Washington when . . .

. . . nobody's ever accused you of something you didn't do.

. . . you're holding a Big Mac and fries, and President Clinton just jogs right by you.

. . . you show up to the debate and
the other guy wins by default.

. . . you're a guy trying to pick up
chicks with JFK Jr.

. . . you're visiting the Vietnam War
Memorial and discover your own
name.

. . . you've been an elected official
for years and still no lobbyist has
approached you with a bribe.

. . . you're running for re-election
and your supporters make up
buttons that read
"Re-elect What's-His-Face."

. . . you're the second guest on
"Larry King Live."

. . . you're the ruler of a small Central American country that's just declared war on the U.S. and you still can't get your phone calls returned.

. . . Ronald Reagan didn't remember you before he had Alzheimer's.

. . . your motorcade is one car long . . . and you're driving it.

. . . your approval rating is higher
than your disapproval rating.

. . . no one asks you to contribute to
their campaign.

. . . you're invited to hear the President's State of the Union address . . . on the radio.

. . . you can't even buy your way into an election.

. . . you fly coach.

. . . you're the only one without a theory on the JFK assassination.

You know you're anonymous in
Washington when . . .

. . . Oliver Stone doesn't want to
make a film about you.

. . . you vote to save the spotted
owl, and the next thing you know,
it's extinct.

. . . Alfonse D'Amato doesn't even want to investigate you.

. . . you have photos of Bob Dole using his right hand and no one wants to buy them.

. . . you still have skeletons in your closet.

. . . you're a half-brother of Bill Clinton who hasn't been found by "Hard Copy" yet.

. . . the government uses your home as a safe house for Salman Rushdie.

. . . Clarence Thomas doesn't want to put a pubic hair on your Coke.

. . . you have your own monument and you still can't get a date.

. . . Bill Clinton hasn't offered to show you *his* Washington Monument (if you know what I mean).

. . . Ross Perot was going to choose
you as his running mate . . .
and didn't.

. . . the last quote you got was
"Four score and seven years
ago . . ."

. . . you always vote for
Lyndon LaRouche.

. . . Newt's mom won't tell you she
thinks Hillary's a bitch.

... you're the incumbent and people still put you as a write-in candidate.

... Jesse Jackson doesn't have a rhyme for your name.

. . . all your campaign contributions
are legal.

. . . you write a book and *you* don't
even know who you are.

You know you're anonymous in
Washington when . . .

. . . the only way you can get on "Meet The Press" is by calling in on the phone lines.

. . . you haven't passed out drunk on the Kennedy Compound lawn.

. . . you were part of the Clinton travel office and you still have a job.

. . . Steve Forbes didn't run a negative ad about you.

. . . AA won't let you join because it's redundant.

. . . you go on ''Crossfire'' and nobody argues.

. . . you have a surefire stock tip to turn one dollar into a million and Lamar Alexander won't take your call.

. . . you have a medical note from your doctor proving you are a congenital liar but still can't get press in William Safire's column.

. . . you have a case of Popov vodka
and Boris Yelstin never stops by.

. . . you can hold your campaign
rallies in public phone booths.

. . . the best inside information you can get is that Marion Barry *may* have had a drug problem.

. . . you offer to be someone's "Deep Throat" and get arrested for solicitation.

. . . you have ten great makeover
tips and Janet Reno doesn't
want them.

. . . no one wants your memoirs . . .
including your own family.

. . . Mike Wallace hasn't seen fit to pester you about that "loan" you took from the tobacco lobby.

. . . Socks the cat has more security than you.

You know you're anonymous in
Washington when . . .

. . . the only White House leaks you hear about are in the faucets.

. . . even dancing naked on Pennsylvania Avenue doesn't get you mentioned on Mark Russell's comedy special.

... you go to visit a fellow
Congressman and a guard says,
"Sir, please stay with the tour."

. . . you send a speech of yours to CNN and they forward it to "America's Funniest Home Videos."

. . . you swipe top-secret CIA information and the only country that will buy it from you is Bermuda.

. . . the best seat you can get for a White House press conference is in your car.

. . . you're second in command but still have to wear an "I'm With the President" T-shirt.

. . . none of your important papers has gone through a shredder yet.

. . . you go on "Face the Nation" and you have to wear a name tag.

. . . you take a foreign dignitary out to lunch and the only table you can get is at Burger King.

. . . even "off the record" people tell you "no comment."

. . . the person swearing you into office has your name written on the back of his hand . . . just in case.

. . . your response to negative ads is, "I know you are, but what am I?"

. . . the best endorsement you can get for your candidacy is from your mom.

... Janet Reno has more secret
admirers than you do.

... you spoke to Hillary Clinton the
night Vince Foster died and you
still haven't gotten a
Congressional subpoena.

You know you're anonymous in
Washington when . . .

. . . the best news program you can get on is "This Week with *Christie* Brinkley."

. . . you end your campaign for President and no other candidate tries to pick up your endorsement.

. . . you're found with a hooker and it's more damaging to her career than yours.

. . . you check the *Who's Who* of Washington and you're not in it.

. . . you're convicted of a federal crime and they send you to a *real* prison.

. . . they give you your own memorial and you're not even dead yet.

. . . the only classified information you can see is in the *Washington Post* personal ads.

. . . the only person you've ever called "Mister President" is Sy Sperling of the Hair Club for Men.

. . . your name on the list of dignitaries at an event comes right after Sonny Bono's.

. . . you've starred in seventeen porno videos and Clarence Thomas doesn't know your on-screen nickname.

. . . the last time you got your name in the paper, Strom Thurmond was going through puberty.

. . . the only time you've ever lied on an official document is when you put down your weight as 165 on your driver's license.

. . . you're the fourth man to say you're running for President and the papers still call it a three-man race.

. . . Rush Limbaugh hasn't said anything derogatory about you.

. . . you're a hot-looking babe and
Candice Gingrich doesn't
want you.

. . . you go to pick up your check
for *Primary Colors* and have no
proof of identification.

. . . the only breach of security you
can commit is by forgetting
the code to your in-home
security system.

. . . the FBI doesn't plant bugs in
your office.

You know you're anonymous in
Washington when . . .

. . . David Duke picks you as his running mate and you're a black Chinese Jew.

. . . no one on "Saturday Night Live" does a lame impression of you.

. . . you support a ban on assault weapons and don't even make the militia's "Most Wanted" list.

. . . the only sub-committee members you know work at Subway.

. . . Bill Clinton doesn't want to feel
your pain.

. . . you stand next to Al Gore and
nobody notices.

. . . the closest you can get to inside information is by watching C-SPAN.

. . . you don't have enough supporters to join MCI's Friends and Family program.

. . . Patti Davis Reagan hasn't offered to get naked in front of you.

. . . the only top-secret thing you can get access to is that really bad movie starring Val Kilmer.

. . . you can be part of an
investigative committee
investigating yourself.

. . . you don't even remember to
vote for yourself.

. . . you're a Democrat in a
Republican Congress.

. . . you're in this country illegally
and Pat Buchanan doesn't care.

. . . Socks the cat bites you and Chelsea asks if you need a doctor. When you reply that you don't she says, "I was talking to the cat."

. . . You're bumped from appearing on "Politically Incorrect" so they can get the government insights on Pauly Shore instead.

. . . you have to change your name to ''None of the Above'' just to get some votes.

. . . your campaign stops only need to happen when you have to go to the bathroom.

You know you're anonymous in
Washington when . . .

. . . Millie the dog won't even hump
your leg.

. . . you're an openly gay man and
you work for Pat Buchanan.

. . . you're a half-brother of the President and you still can't get a record deal.

. . . the school they name after you is called "What's His Name High."

. . . the government shuts down and no one notices you're gone.

. . . the only media coverage your campaign gets is from New York's PS 137.

... the only place you can get your ads to run is on cable access.

... your nomination to the Supreme Court goes through without a hitch.

... the only government experience you can claim is being president of your fifth-grade class.

... instead of bringing you your schedule in the morning your secretary brings you her shopping list.

... you have to raise money for your campaign by selling lemonade on your front lawn.

... the gangs don't even bother to shoot at you when they drive by.

. . . Lloyd Bentsen says to you "You're no Jack Kennedy. You're not even Dan Quayle. In fact, I have no idea who you are."

. . . your last public broadcast included the phrase "Please drive forward for your order."

. . . men would rather ogle the woman standing next to you on the subway . . . and that woman's Janet Reno.

. . . your attempt to speak freely to the youth of America involves talking into the clown's mouth.

. . . the only magazine cover you get during your campaign is on *Skateboarders Weekly*.

. . . the only supporters you have are in your underwear drawer.

You know you're anonymous in
Washington when . . .

. . . a survey says that you have 0% of the vote with a margin of error of $\pm$ 0%.

. . . the average citizen has more influence than you do.

. . . you have to pay your own
health insurance.

. . . more people drink Billy Beer
than have heard of you.

. . . your barnstorming campaign
only has stops at real barns.

. . . people ask you how you're
doing in the polls, and you think
they mean the North and South.

. . . there's no photo of you shaking hands with an alien on the cover of the *Weekly World News*.